Table of Contents

Introduction
Color Yourself Calm: Mindful Art Enhancement

Coloring books can help reintroduce art as an important component of health and wellness. As such, it might be helpful to think of coloring books as a sort of creativity starter kit. It can help get your mind working in a creative way and give you a taste of all the benefits artistic expression can bring. This is particularly helpful for people who aren't comfortable with more expressive forms of art because coloring can provide a structured way for them to feel engaged with the art process without the pressure to create something from a blank page.

While reading, music, and sports have plenty of health benefits, coloring has the unique ability to engage your fine motor skills while training the brain to focus. Coloring can offer the additional benefit of mindfulness, or being in the moment. Coloring is calming, as moving your hand in a rhythmic fashion can become a form of meditation. As a result, coloring releases tension and reduces stress and anxiety. Coloring also provides crucial time away from screens and technology, which lets your brain rest and reset. This coloring book is designed to help you reconnect as you color illustrations of the physical, emotional, intellectual, social, spiritual, occupational, and environmental dimensions of wellness. Be mindful of ways you can improve each dimension of wellness as you color.

Interesting Color Facts

Adult Coloring Books Are Bestsellers · In April of 2015, CNN reported that five of the top ten bestselling books on Amazon were adult coloring books. In just one year, Nielsen Bookscan estimated that sales jumped from 1 million adult coloring books sold in 2014 to 12 million in 2015. The catalyst for the craze was the work of Scottish author Johanna Basford, whose 2013 title, "Secret Garden: An Inky Treasure Hunt and Coloring Book" began burning up bestseller lists.

Adult Coloring Books Are Big Business · Nielsen reported that total sales of colored pencils shot up 26.3% in 2015, a sharp increase compared to the previous three years, when growth ranged from 1.3% to 7.2%. The strong demand for adult coloring books and artist supplies has also impacted the total annual sales of big chains such as Barnes & Noble, Walmart, Target, and Michaels, who have all chosen to stock a wide variety of adult coloring book titles. In fact, Michaels has expanded its assortment to more than 150 adult coloring books!

Media Coverage Of The Adult Coloring Book Trend · Stories run on adult coloring books in the last few years have been published in major news outlets including The New York Times, The Washington Post, The Wall Street Journal, The New Yorker, Los Angeles Times, Boston Globe, Time Magazine, Forbes, CNN, Good Morning America, USA Today, and ABC News, as well as many local news sources.

Coloring Benefits
The Science On The Benefits Of Adult Coloring Books Is Emerging · Although the science on the benefits of art therapy, creativity, and crafting on a variety of physical and mental health benefits are more well established in the scientific literature, research

evidence on the specific benefits of adult coloring books is still in its beginning stages. As such, it may take some time to reach more conclusive evidence of its effect. Dr. Pearson from the University of New South Wales Sydney says, "It's one of those situations where the general public is moving faster than science ... and it will take time to run the studies and write up the papers." However, despite its recent emergence, several studies on adult coloring books have been published documenting preliminary effects.

More Relaxed · Researchers have observed changes in the heart rate and brainwaves of people as they color, suggesting that coloring can impact important physiological changes associated with relaxation. Dr. Stan Rodski, a neuropsychologist, speculated that this positive impact on physiological health could come from the ways coloring draws the brain's attention away from troubling thoughts and worries as well as the benefits of repetitive motor activity. Structured, rhythmic endeavors such as coloring, knitting, crocheting or quilting have been found to release serotonin—a neurotransmitter related to feelings of well-being, happiness, and relaxation.

Decreased Stress · Research investigating the impact of visual art-making on healthy adults found that making art resulted in statistically significant lower cortisol levels (stress hormone) as well as feelings of relaxation and enjoyment. Other studies with college students have found similar reductions in stress or tension from coloring for just 20 minutes or participating in a creative arts intervention during class. It is possible that self-soothing activities (such as coloring) can help calm down or relax the amygdala part of our brain that can keep individuals in a heightened state of stressful fear, worry, or panic. Coloring may help turn that response down by giving your amygdala periodic rests as well as help retrain your amygdala to respond less harshly to stress when it does happen.

Coloring Strategies To Try

Invest In A Quality Colored Pencil Brand · Not all colored pencils are the same. Cheap colored pencils tend to have harder wax leads and less pigment which mean they break more often, produce less vibrant colors, and have a tendency to leave some white spaces in the grain of the paper. Mid-range pencils (from brands like Staedtler or Faber Castel) offer a softer application. This allows you to get more vibrant color on the paper, experiment with some simple shading and blending techniques, and produce significantly better results than bargain bin pencils.

Experiment With Art Supplies Before Buying · Find the biggest art store in town and experiment with their colored pencils to see which ones you like the feel of. Most higher-end brands offer single pencils you can "test drive" before you decide what set you may like to purchase. After experimenting with various brands, it is best to buy the biggest set of colored pencils that you can afford because it ends up being cheaper than buying a small box of 12 or 24 and then filling in with singles. If you find a particular color you love that is not included in a set, you can usually buy individual pencils one at a time.

Test Any Markers Or Gel Pens Before Coloring · Before you begin coloring with markers or gel pens, test them on a blank page in the coloring book to see if it bleeds through the page. This is especially important for coloring books with double sided pages.

Color Corner

I found I could say things with color and shapes that I couldn't say any other way—things I had no words for.
Georgia O'Keeffe

Color is a power which directly influences the soul.
Wassily Kandinsky

Mere color, unspoiled by meaning, and unallied with definite form, can speak to the soul in a thousand different ways.
Oscar Wilde

Section 1
Physical Health

Things you can do to boost physical health

- Eat healthy, nutritious food
- Drink plenty of water
- Don't skip meals; breakfast is especially important
- Cut back on sugar and salt
- Get enough sleep; seven hours a night is considered optimal
- Exercise regularly to stay in shape and to build immunity
- Avoid addictive substances and recreational drugs
- Get regular physical exams
- See a doctor if you develop symptoms
- Don't overuse or misuse prescription medications

Interesting Color Facts

Interest In Adult Coloring Books Elicit A Statement From The American Art Therapy Association · The American Art Therapy Association issued a statement in 2015 supporting the use of coloring books for "pleasure and self-care" but cautioned that they should not be confused with professional art therapy sessions. Art therapy sessions involve a creative process inherent to art-making that occurs within a relationship with a credentialed art therapist who can assist clients in tapping into their internal experience in ways that evoke emotions to guide a therapeutic intervention.

Adult Coloring Books Are Not Art Therapy, But They Can Be Therapeutic · Drena Fagen, an art therapist and adjunct instructor at New York University's Steinhardt School sums this up nicely when she makes an important distinction, "I don't consider the coloring books as art therapy. I consider the coloring books therapeutic, which is not the same thing."

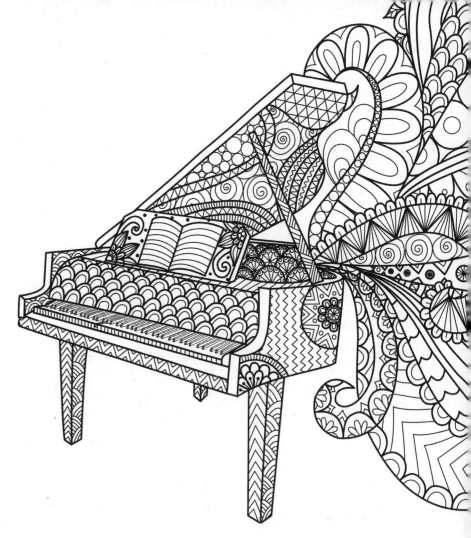

People Who Like To Color May Reap The Most Benefits · People who like to color tend to reap the strongest benefit from the practice. For example, researchers found that people who liked ongoing mindfulness guidance while coloring displayed an increase in mindfulness and a decrease in anxiety after coloring whereas those who didn't like it evidenced no such effect. This suggests that the willingness to do, and fondness for the practice had a vast effect on the outcome. Thus, the potential of positive outcomes associated with coloring may be dependent upon the liking of those practices in the first place. Health psychologist, Nancy Mramor agrees. She says, "Somebody might feel a wonderful relaxation just sitting and coloring, while someone else might find it's not at all what they wanted." Thus, adult coloring books may not be for everyone, and caution should be exercised in forcing people into practices that are not enjoyed.

Coloring Benefits

Decreased Anxiety · Several research studies have documented a decrease in anxiety levels when people color with some research indicating that coloring certain designs (such as mandalas) can reduce anxiety levels significantly more than coloring other designs (plaid) or simply free-coloring on a blank piece of paper. Researchers speculate that coloring allows us to switch our brains from focusing on troublesome or worrisome thoughts to focusing on deciding how to color the various shapes, sizes, and edges of a pattern in front of us. This new focus could occupy the same parts of the brain involved in creating the anxiety and stop the anxiety-related mental imagery or thought processes from emerging.

Reduced Depressive Symptoms · University students who participated in a week-long coloring intervention showed significantly lower levels of depressive symptoms immediately afterwards. This suggests that daily coloring can improve negative psychological outcomes and may provide an effective, inexpensive, and highly accessible self-help tool. The reduction in depressive symptoms is likely due to the reward center in the brain releasing dopamine (a natural anti-depressant) when you do something pleasurable such

Color
Corner

Life is about using the whole box of crayons.
RuPaul

The soul becomes dyed with the colors of its thoughts
Marcus Aurelius

Nature always wears the colors of the spirit.
Ralph Waldo Emerson

as coloring. Other related research has found that creative crafts can also alleviate depression. For example, one study of more than 3,500 knitters found that 81% of respondents with depression reported feeling happy after knitting.

Improved Mood · Several studies have observed improved moods and emotions in participants who color, with one study documenting a significant reduction in negative mood states after only 20 minutes of coloring. Coloring certain patterns (such as circular mandala drawings) has been found to be particularly effective in improving mood. It is speculated that art-making can help elevate your mood by distracting your mind from negative thoughts and feelings through a focus on bright colors and happy images.

Coloring Strategies To Try
Color With A Blank Piece Of Paper Behind The Page · Colored pencils will easily pick up even the smallest dents, divots, or textures of the surface you are working on. Adding one or two blank pieces of paper behind the page you are coloring not only gives you a smoother coloring surface, but also helps protect the pages behind it from denting or the design being damaged if you have a heavy hand or are using markers or gel pens.

Slow Down · Be patient and take your time. Colored pencils require a slow and meticulous approach. If you go into your drawing with this in mind, then your chances of success are greatly improved. Enjoy the process—you will be happier with your coloring.

Draw and color your physical strength.

Section 2
Emotional Health

Things you can do to improve emotional health

- Look for the positive, both overall and in particular situations
- Be aware of your strengths, weaknesses, and limitations
- Learn to express yourself appropriately
- Set priorities and address top priorities first
- Share your feelings, even those that are difficult
- Learn to manage stress effectively
- Build strong networks with family, friends, peers, and students
- Tune into your feelings

Interesting Color Facts

The Physics Of Seeing In Color · The human eye can only see the visible light spectrum composed of electromagnetic radiation at certain wavelengths.   Sir Isaac Newton was the first to discover that pure white light (sunlight) was composed of the visible colors in the rainbow when he passed it through a prism in 1666. Each color of the rainbow is composed of specific wavelengths and quantities of energy. The cones in our eyes can translate these wavelengths into color in the presence of light. When light shines on an object, some colors bounce off the object and others are absorbed by it. Our eyes only see the colors that are bounced off, or reflected.

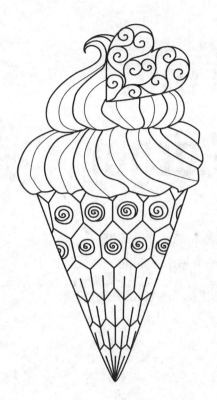

Color Therapy · Using color as medicine to cure diseases is a centuries old concept that was practiced in ancient Egypt, Greece, China, and India as early as 2,000 B.C. The ancient Egyptians and Greeks used colored minerals, stones, crystals, salves, and dyes as remedies for specific diseases as did more contemporary 19th-century color healers who claimed to cure everything from constipation to meningitis with colored glass filters. Despite color therapy's long history, there is little scientific evidence to prove its efficacy. The current scientific study of the effects of light on humans has replaced the term chromotherapy with the term photobiology in an effort to distance itself from color therapy's associations with mysticism, color symbolism, and magic.

Caveat On Color Research · Because the scientific literature on the impact of color on psychological functioning can be provocative and media friendly it is tempting to make claims that may not reflect the complexity and contradictions found in the developing science. Color psychology is a uniquely complex area of inquiry; as such, patience and prudence regarding the findings, conclusions, and real-world applications should be exercised. Although there is considerable promise in this research, more theoretical and empirical work needs to be done.

Coloring Benefits

Better Overall Health · Numerous studies have examined how making crafts benefits mood and physical health. In a 2006 study co-sponsored by the National Endowment for the Arts and several federal health agencies, researchers found that adults 65 or older who engaged in creative activities such as making jewelry, painting, or writing had better overall health, made fewer visits to the doctor, used less medication, and had fewer health problems than non-crafters. "There's promising evidence coming out to support what a lot of crafters have known anecdotally for quite some time," says Catherine Carey Levisay, a clinical neuropsychologist, "and that's that creating -- whether it be through art, music, cooking, quilting, sewing, drawing, photography (or) cake decorating -- is beneficial to us in a number of important ways." Although this study did not specifically assess the impact of coloring, it could be argued coloring would fit within the creative activities explored.

Reduced Risk Of Cognitive Impairment · Neuroscientist have found that leisure activities such as playing games, reading books, or crafting can reduce your chances of developing mild cognitive impairment by 30% to 50%. It is hypothesized that purposeful and meaningful activities such as cooking, music, drawing, photography, knitting, meditation, reading, or arts and crafts could counter the effects of stress-related diseases and reduce the risk of Alzheimer's or

Color Corner

dementia. These creative activities can build up a cognitive reserve which can ultimately protect people from cognitive impairment through stimulating the neurological system, countering the effects of stress-related diseases, and enhancing health and well-being. Although this study did not specifically assess the impact of coloring, it could be argued coloring would fit within the creative craft activities assessed.

Potential For Increased Mindfulness · Studies have consistently shown that people who engage in mindfulness meditation practices experience a wide variety of health benefits. Although many mandala coloring books are being promoted as "mindfulness" coloring books, research indicates the coloring books as they currently exist and are typically used by consumers do not produce states of mindfulness. However, these same researchers argue it is reasonable to imagine coloring books could be a useful mindfulness tool if the act of coloring were paired with the right guidance and intentions. For example, while coloring, the intention to be attentive and aware of the present moment in an accepting and non-judgmental manner could be achieved with ongoing guidance and instruction. In fact, researchers found that participants who enjoyed participating in mindfulness guidance while coloring displayed an increase in state mindfulness afterwards. Other interventions that pair art therapy with a mindfulness practice have found a significant decrease in symptoms of distress and improvements in key aspects of health-related quality of life indicating the potential benefits of such approaches.

Coloring Strategies To Try

Obtain Brighter Results With Layers · Once you have mastered coloring between the lines with an even pressure, you can take the same pencil and go back over that coloring again to provide a second or even third layer of color. Applying extra layers of color will remove some of the white grain that was missed in the first layer and bring depth to your color. If you mix up the direction you color each layer, you can produce a smoother finish. Always remember to hold the pencil sideways so the greatest area of the tip is in contact with the paper.

Experiment With Pressure Shading · The simplest, most natural type of shading is to just alter pressure on your pencil. Pushing harder on your page will result in a darker color and pushing lighter on the page will give you a lighter color. You can begin by shading the entire area smoothly in the lightest value, and then add more layers and pressure to the areas you want shaded. Pressing harder can intensify, but not darken a color. Remember that although it is tempting to put lots of pressure on the pencil to produce the darkest color, too much pressure will likely cause you to break your pencil leads.

Try A Colorless Blender · A pencil or marker colorless blender can be used to produce a burnished (polished, shiny, or buffed) look to your coloring. It is best to start in the lightest area and press hard while making slightly larger overlapping short or circular marks. This will darken and intensify the color, smooth out all the white specks, and give a polished surface to the area. If you don't have a colorless blender, a light pencil (white or cream) can be applied over the area with heavy pressure to burnish. This approach does result in a slightly lighter finished color, however, due to the white application. Alternatively, you can also try burnishing with solvents such as alcohol applied over the colored pencil layer with a soft brush.

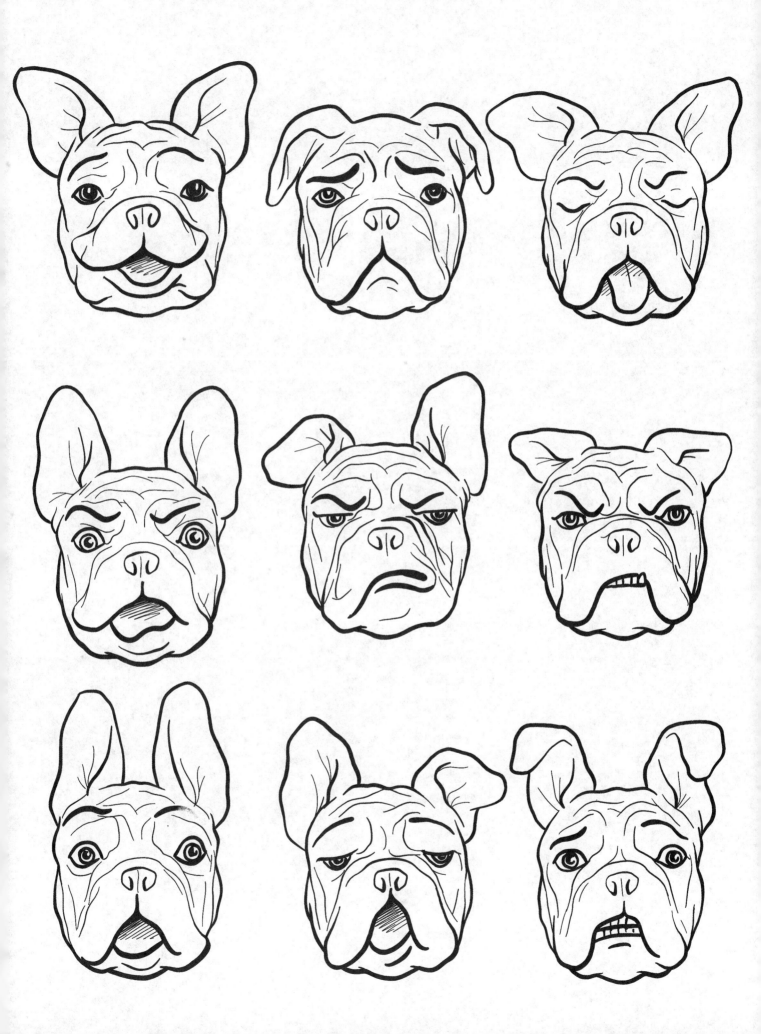

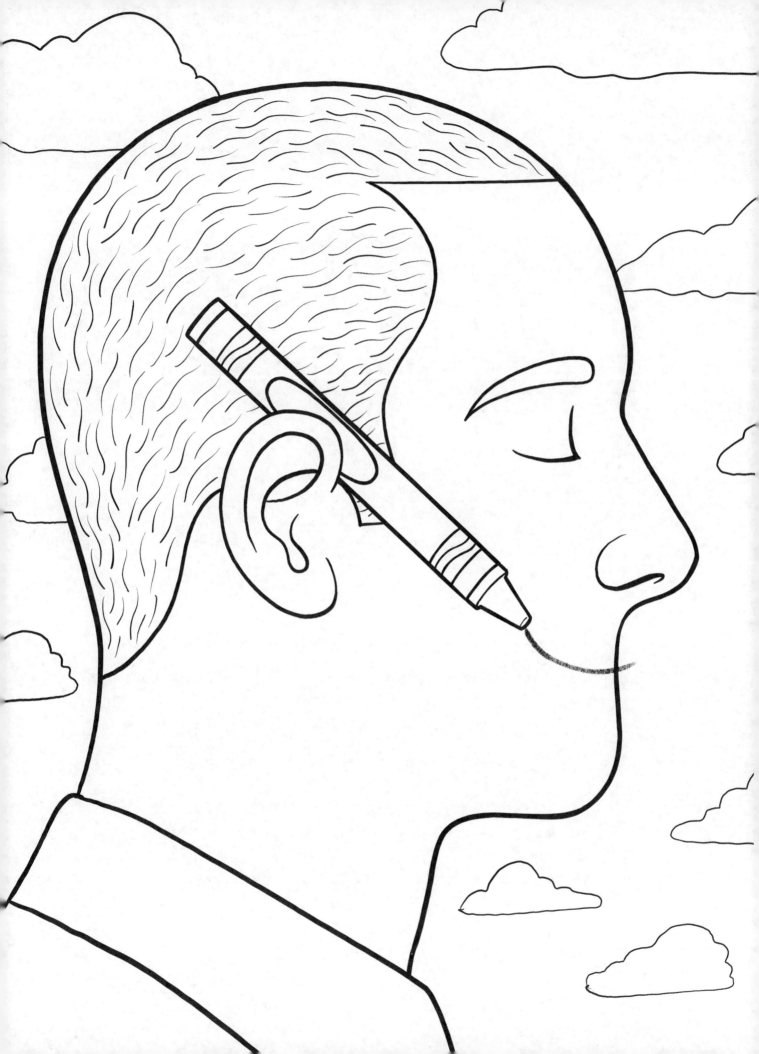

Draw and color your emotional strength.

Section 3
Intellectual Health

Things you can do to improve intellectual health

- Approach new opportunities with an open mind
- Take advantage of the chance to learn new things
- Actively seek challenges
- Set challenging but realistic goals
- Seek stimulation and mental growth
- Get involved in cultural experiences
- Bring new ideas and methods to the table
- Never stop learning

Interesting Color Facts

Favorite Color · Preferences for certain colors are highly individual and subjective because they are influenced by social learning, culture, and personal experiences. As such, it would be very difficult to determine a universally favorite color. However, if one had to pick one, Steve Palmer (professor emeritus at the University of California, Berkeley and expert on visual perception and color preference) would say blue. "Cross-culturally, the most highly favored color is a very saturated blue" because it is associated with things that are almost always good such as a deep, clean lake, a clear sky, or a beautiful sapphire gemstone.

History Of Color Associations With Emotion · Goethe first penned his theorizing on color and psychological functioning in 1810 with his work titled "Theory of Colors" where he linked color categories (colors of yellow, red—yellow, yellow—red) to emotional responses such as warmth and excitement.

Variable Impact Of Color On Feelings, Moods, And Emotions · Science has long recognized a link between color and mood and despite a large body of scientific research on this, the results are often inconclusive or contradictory. This is most likely due to the fact that our emotional responses to color are closely tied to our personal, social and cultural color preferences which are subjective. Consequently, the same color can elicit positive or negative feelings in different people depending on what is associated with that color. The same color can also elicit different responses within the same person depending on its context. For example, blue on a ribbon can elicit feelings of pride and accomplishment for winning first place, but blue on a steak could elicit feelings of disgust because it indicates rot. As a general rule, because color is so dependent on personal experience and context, it is impossible to be universally translated to specific associations with distinct feelings or emotions.

Coloring Benefits

Pathway To Increased Mindfulness · If approached and guided properly, coloring books could become a useful tool in contemporary secular mindfulness programs designed to develop attentional training, open awareness, and a focus on the present moment. Given the current public engagement with coloring books, this could be a good way to introduce people to the benefits of mindfulness practices and help benefit overall community health.

Increased Flow · If you enjoy creative projects, you have probably experienced flow, or the tendency to become so absorbed in what you are doing that you lose track of time and are able to momentarily forget about your worries, obligations, or even physical pain. Scholars hypothesize that the benefits of coloring may be related to its ability to create a flow state. In fact, research has found that people who participate in art-making sessions report a sense of flow and of losing themselves in their work. According to Csikszentmihalyi, flow is the secret to happiness. "When we are involved in [creativity], we feel that we are living more fully

Color Corner

Colors express the main psychic functions of man.
Carl Gustav Jung

Color is a matter of taste and of sensitivity.
Edouard Manet

One can speak poetry just by arranging colors well.
Vincent Van Gogh

than during the rest of life ... Your sense of time disappears. You forget yourself. You feel part of something larger."

Increased Self-Awareness, Authenticity And Psychological Well-Being · Art-making sessions have been found to be helpful in learning about new aspects of one's self. For example, researchers found that students who drew and interpreted mandalas scored significantly higher on measures of authenticity, awareness, psychological well-being, and personal growth than students who did not. It is hypothesized that the creative process of making mandalas helps individuals experience and reflect on the essence of who they are. This is an old tradition; Carl Jung believed mandalas served as expressions of the self and one's identity and used mandalas to help his patients access their subconscious and create new self-knowledge. Although coloring pre-drawn mandalas may be different, it is possible that it could lead to similar levels of introspection with the proper guidance.

Coloring Strategies To Try

Layer Different Colors To Create Shadows And Highlights · Layering darker colors over light or medium ones adds depth and darkens, while its opposite (layering light or medium colors over dark colors) burnishes and adds nuances without dramatic changes. Both techniques produce colors that are more natural in their appearance. Experiment with layering related or similar colors (such as purple over red) as well as completely opposite colors. Sticking to black and white for all of your shadow and highlight needs can leave a picture looking flat. For richer shadows, try using dark browns, blues, or purples before using black to darken a color and avoid leaving black as the top layer of any color. To lighten a color, layer over it with a lighter hue of the same color or experiment with very pale golds and yellows for warmer highlights before resorting to white.

Try Mixing Colors · Instead of reaching for the manufactured green, mix your own by layering blue and yellow. You can always go over the application with a manufactured green, but the color will appear more natural as the yellows and blues show through. Adjusting the pressure when mixing colors affects the intensity and resulting color. Experiment as you work to find the right combinations of pressure to produce the colors and values that you want. You can practice this technique by shading two contrasting colors into one another. For example, take your red pencil and shade from left to right, dark to light. Next, take your green pencil and shade from right to left, dark to light. Work on blending them as seamlessly as possible where they meet in the middle.

Experiment With The Direction Of Your Strokes · Just as brush strokes in a painting can inform the viewer of the form and texture of the subject, the direction of the marks made with the pencil can do the same. If you're not sure which direction the strokes should be pulled, just consider the cross contours of the form of the subject. By pulling strokes to align with the cross contours of the form, you can communicate a bit more to the viewer. If you pull the strokes in a direction that contradicts the cross contours, you could make your drawing look flat.

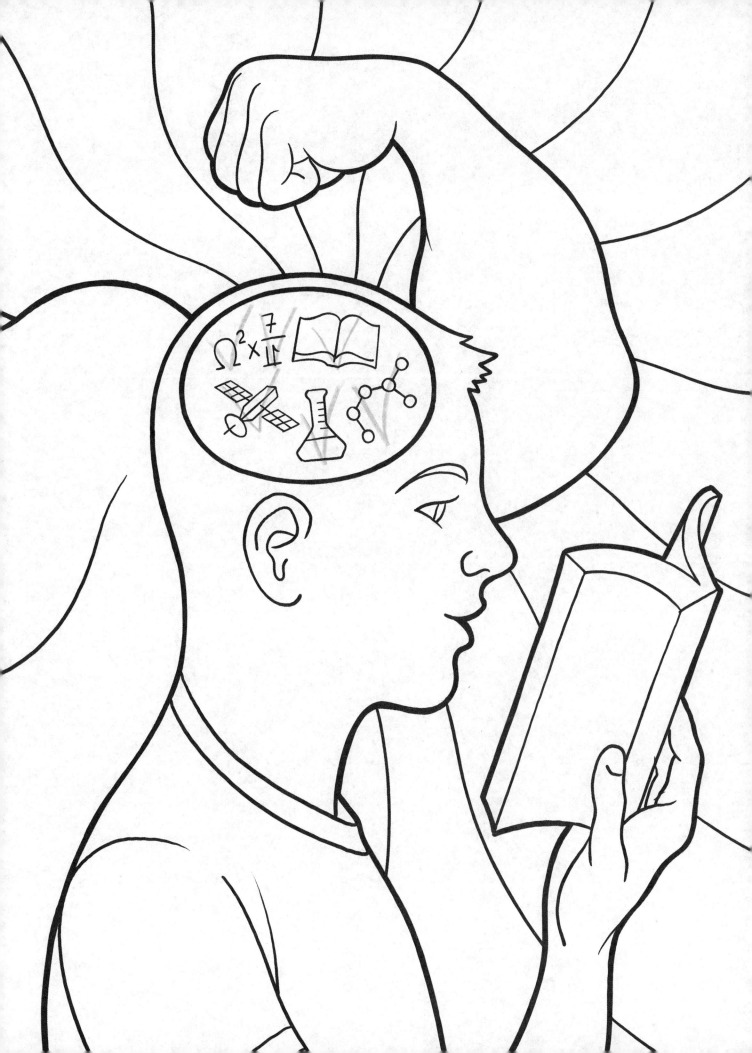

Draw and color your intellectual strength.

Section 4
Social Health

Things you can do to improve social health

- Improve your ability to interact with other people
- Build your self-image so you feel comfortable among others
- Be receptive to the ideas and experiences of others
- Use empathy to help you understand others
- Build networks among diverse types of people
- Seek to make new friends and establish professional contacts
- Work to understand various cultural norms
- Become committed to the common welfare of your school or community

Interesting Color Facts

The Impact Of Color On Consumer Purchases · Color can exert a powerful influence on the objects people choose to purchase, the clothes they wear, and the way they decorate their homes. People often select objects in colors that evoke certain moods or feelings with one study finding that up to 90% of snap judgments made about products are based on color alone.

The Impact Of Color On Food And Beverage Perception · Color has been found to play a key role in food choices by influencing taste thresholds, sweetness perception, food preference, pleasantness, and acceptability. For example, by changing the color of a food, one can maintain the perception that the food is sweet, despite the fact you have reduced its sugar content. Color can also interfere with being able to correctly identify distinct flavors and judgments of flavor intensity and profiles which has been shown to dramatically influence the taste, pleasantness and acceptability of foods. For example, the color red has been shown to influence food and beverage perception and consumption. One study found that people liked the flavor of wine best when they consumed it under red versus green or white lighting despite the fact that it was the exact same type of wine in each setting.

The Impact Of Color On Food Consumption · Several sensory cues affect food intake including appearance, taste, color, odor, texture, temperature, and flavor. Although taste is an important factor in regulating food intake, in most cases, the first sensory contact with food is through the eyes. One study identified how various visual factors associated with food such as its color, portion size, shape, number, and volume impacted food consumption in the hopes they could be manipulated to increase fruit and vegetable intake in children and decrease excessive food intake in adults. Another study found that by manipulating the ambience or social context within which food was eaten, they could also alter the amount of food consumed. They found changes in food intake when they altered eating locations, food color, ambient temperatures, lighting, temperature of foods, smell of food, time of consumption, number of people there, and ambient sounds. It is possible that by manipulating these ambient factors (including the color of the food and the color of the room and its lighting) one may also be able to alter food intake.

Coloring Benefits

Reduced Screen Time · For people who feel they have too many screens in their lives and are interested in the idea of unplugging, coloring may be the perfect solution. Part of the appeal of coloring is the tactile nature of the books and colored pencils which offers respite to the screen-weary. "People are really excited to do something analog and creative, at a time when we're all so overwhelmed by screens and the Internet," says Johanna Basford, a Scottish illustrator, "and coloring is not as scary as a blank sheet of paper or canvas. It's a great way to de-stress."

Increased Playfulness · Making time for play as an adult has been associated with a broad range of positive outcomes such as academic success, coping with stress, better physical health, increased self-esteem, innovative work performance and productivity, increased social support, and better subjective well-being. Thus, doing activities that help you engage playfully with the world can be beneficial and even necessary for optimal well-being. Coloring can be a form of play. It may take you back to a simpler and happier

Color Corner

I would like to paint the way a bird sings.

Claude Monet

Color in a picture is like enthusiasm in life.

Vincent van Gogh

Color—what a deep and mysterious language—the language of dreams.

Paul Gauguin

time of childhood when you didn't have as many responsibilities and could just do something for the pure joy of it. Tapping into this experience can be a cathartic and enjoyable way to bring you out of your present stresses and worries.

Creative Starter Kit · Coloring books can help reintroduce art as an important component of health and wellness. As such, it might be helpful to think of coloring books as a sort of creativity starter kit. It can help get your mind working in a creative way and give you a taste of all the benefits artistic expression can bring. This is particularly helpful for people who aren't comfortable with more expressive forms of art because coloring can provide a structured way for them to feel engaged with the art process without the pressure to create something from a blank page. The American Art Therapy Association states, "coloring books provide a controlled, contained use of art for self-soothing purposes, and their success-oriented nature is conducive to fulfillment of the need for instant gratification. They can be completed by anyone with minimal risk. Preprinted designs allow for structure that facilitates safety and minimizes emotional risk which may explain their appeal to broader audiences."

Coloring Strategies To Try

Create Coloring Spaces You Find Relaxing · There is no wrong way to color for relaxation. You can color nearly anywhere - on planes, in front of the TV, in coffee shops, or during a therapy session. They key is to find or create a space you enjoy. For example, you might discover you like to color in a quiet room filled with natural light while you listen to your favorite music.

Choose Coloring Supplies That Fit Best With Your Needs · If you have arthritis or carpal tunnel wrist problems, try coloring with markers instead of pencils because they require less pressure and are much easier on your hands to use.

Experiment With Creative Effects · Try using a white colored pencil or crayon to randomly color over areas of your image. When you apply a watercolor wash over the top, the paint will resist the areas colored in, leaving you with a cool, distressed effect on your page. Alternatively, you can try shading with regular pencil on your coloring book image. It will make it look less like a coloring book image, and more like a hand drawing.

Draw and color your social strength.

Section 5
Spiritual Health

Things you can do to improve spiritual health

- Make sure your actions and decisions are consistent with your values
- Be tolerant of the views of others
- Spend time thinking about your purpose in life
- Set aside time each day to do those things that increase your spirituality—pray, meditate, take a walk in nature, listen to beautiful music, or do volunteer work
- Spend time each day just being quiet or relaxing and thinking outside yourself

Interesting Color Facts

The Impact Of Color On Children's Candy Selections · A study gave 120 children aged 5-9 choices among three types of candy in 5 different colors and found that children preferred candy that was red, green, orange or yellow, in that order.

The Impact Of Color On Perceived Drug Effectiveness · The color of placebo pills has been found to influence the perceived effectiveness of a drug with warm-colored placebo pills reported as more effective than cool-colored placebo pills.

The Impact Of Color Names On Consumer Choices · Researchers found that when people were asked to evaluate products such as makeup, clothing, or food with different color names, the "fancy" color names were preferred far more often. For example, brown eye shadow labelled as "mocha" instead of "brown" or jelly beans labeled as "razzmatazz" instead of "lemon yellow" were found to be significantly more likeable, and thus more likely to be purchased despite the fact that the products themselves were exactly the same color. Choosing creative, descriptive and memorable names to describe certain colors can be an important part of making sure the color of the product achieves its biggest impact.

Coloring Benefits

Increased Social Networks · Although coloring is usually a solo activity, its recent popularity has turned it into a social one through events like coloring parties, gatherings, clubs, or evenings out. Because you don't need to concentrate very much when you are coloring in a coloring book, you can talk with others and build social networks in a fairly low stress and non-confrontational way.

Identify People Best Suited For Art Therapy · A systematic review of randomized controlled trials on the effectiveness of creative interventions led by art therapists on adults with cancer found evidence that such interventions can help with stress, anxiety, depression, quality of life, mood, coping, and anger. Although coloring in a coloring book does not equate to art therapy, some art therapists have suggested the use of coloring books could help identify those who might benefit most widely from art therapeutic interventions available in professional health care settings and thus help provide more targeted and effective interventions for cancer patients. In addition, because those who judge themselves as bad artists may be more likely to miss out on the benefits of art therapy, some art therapists use coloring as a way to help people begin their creative journey in ways that can bolster their courage enough to try other mediums or forms of art.

Art Therapy, Cancer, And Chronic Illnesses · A variety of art interventions involving activities such as drawing, modeling clay, card making, collage, pottery, acrylics, water color, crocheting, and other crafts have been found to increase positive outcomes for clinical patients struggling with a variety of cancers or chronic illnesses. Benefits include improved well-being, increased social networks, decreased negative emotions, reduced depression, reduced stress, decreased anxiety, increased positive emotions, improved concentration, increased sense of purpose and self-worth, improved flow and spontaneity, decreased symptoms of distress, and other improvements in key aspects of health-related quality of life. Although art therapy interventions are different than creating art on one's own, similar results were found when examining the impact of art-making on cancer patients or people coping with chronic illness and disability in less structured settings—such as people who engaged regularly in art as a leisure activity, or a simple one hour art-making session without an art therapist. This suggests the potential benefits of creativity and art-making for the general public and some of the reasons why coloring may have positive effects.

Coloring Strategies To Try

Try Indenting · Indenting is a technique that can add texture and character to your coloring book pages. Place a sheet of tracing paper over the image and then use a pencil or pen to indent the image. You won't be actually drawing on the image, but rather

Color Corner

Artists are just children
who refused to put down
their crayons.
Al Hirschfeld

You can't use up creativity.
The more you use, the more
you have.
Maya Angelou

Even broken crayons
can still color.
Anonymous

indenting the paper behind it so that when your colored pencil goes over it, it will leave white outlines in the spots you indented.

Try Hatching And Cross Hatching With Ink · When using ink, you can "color" in the page using different pen strokes like hatching and cross hatching and tiny patterns to create an intricate coloring pattern that complements the style of the coloring book page illustrator.

Try Texture Rubbings · Place a textured object (such as coins or leaves) under the coloring book page and then gently shade the space with the side of the colored pencil point to fill in the area. This will add interesting bits of texture to your coloring book page and when used on an entire page, it can create a nice effect.

Draw and color your spiritual strength.

Section 6
Occupational Health

Things you can do to improve occupational health

- Talk openly with your administrator and coworkers
- Do things that help you enjoy your job
- When an occasional "bad day" happens, focus on the positive
- Regularly assess your workload to make sure that what you've been asked to do won't overload you or burn you out
- Schedule in time each day to do something fun or to relax

Interesting Color Facts

The Impact Of Color On Cognitive Tasks · Color has been examined for its impact on learning performance and achievement in a variety of contexts. Red typically has arousal effects which tends to make people pay attention, be more cautious, detail-oriented, and make less errors on certain tasks. For example, one study found that seeing the color red enhanced performance on tests of recall and attention to detail like remembering words or checking spelling and punctuation when compared with seeing the color blue. However, red can also be perceived as distracting when people see it as a waring cue. For example, viewing red prior to a challenging cognitive task (such as a test) has been shown to undermine performance by creating caution and avoidance. People who were shown red test covers before an I.Q. test either did worse than those shown green or neutral colors or chose to answer easier questions, thus reducing their overall score. Likewise, students tend to do better on tests that are on blue instead of red paper.

The Impact Of Color On Creativity · The color blue has been associated with enhanced performance on creative tasks. For example, people who saw the color blue before a test performed better on questions requiring imagination like inventing creative uses for a brick or creating toys from shapes. In addition, blue light has been found to facilitate alertness and enhance performance on tasks requiring sustained attention due to the ways it activates the brain structures involved in sub-cortical arousal and higher-order attentional processing. This has led some people to suggest red rooms for defusing bombs and blue rooms for creative projects.

Impact Of Color On Athletic Performance · Wearing red has been shown to enhance performance and perceived performance in sports competitions and tasks. For example, wearing a red jersey has consistently been associated with a higher probability of winning across a range of sports. Researchers found that evenly matched Olympic athletes who wore red uniforms in boxing, tae kwon do, Greco-Roman wrestling and freestyle wrestling defeated those wearing blue uniforms 60 percent of

Color Corner

Colors are light's
suffering and joy.

Goethe

Why do two colors, put one
next to the other, sing?

Pablo Picasso

Try to be a rainbow in
someone's cloud.

Maya Angelou

the time. It is hypothesized that red may subconsciously symbolize and convey aggressiveness or dominance and lead to a competitive sports advantage. Red has also been found to cause people to react with greater speed and force in motor output when pinching or gripping something which can be useful during athletic activities. Red is not the only color that seems to impact athletic performance. One study found that sports teams that dressed in mostly black uniforms were more likely to receive penalties and be associated with negative qualities such as aggression.

Coloring Benefits

Helps Family Caregivers Cope · Research examined the impact of an art-making class on family caregivers of patients with cancer and found that after participating in a two-hour art-making class, family caregivers showed significantly reduced levels of anxiety and stress. This indicates that art-making can have a therapeutic effect on those who care for the sick and suggests the potential benefits of coloring as a coping mechanism.

Art Therapy And Increased Communication With Dementia Patients · Artistic ability and creative expression can help dementia patients express thoughts and emotions they are experiencing but are unable to express verbally. This increase in non-verbal communication can help provide a better understanding of the patient's needs and development of treatment goals and interventions. "Art therapy is helpful for dementia and Alzheimer's patients," said Dr. Daniel Potts, a neurologist and dementia specialist, "because it enables an individual who is having trouble communicating to bypass the language problems they may be having and communicate and express themselves in a different way." Other research on patients diagnosed with multiple personality/dissociative identity disorder has found similar results. Although this research applies specifically to people with dementia or a mental illness who are working with an art therapist, it is possible that artistic expression found in coloring can provide opportunities for non-verbal expressions of thoughts and emotions in non-clinical populations as well.

Coloring Strategies To Try

Experiment With Color Palettes · There are lots of ways to choose a color. You can browse color palettes on Pinterest boards, copy other artist color palettes, find an image with colors that you love online and upload it to a free online color palette generator, or check out websites designed for people who love color (such as Design Seeds). Different palettes can have different effects. For example, monochromatic palettes in neutral shades such as creams and browns can create an "antiqued" look on your coloring book pages. Alternatively, trendy colors (Pantone releases its trend forecast twice a year) can reflect a more contemporary or "hip" design choice.

Be Social · Look for local coloring groups at your library or art club. Alternatively, if you like to color in public places such as coffee shops, bring an extra coloring book along. You may run into a friend or stranger who is curious and would like to join you when they see what you are doing.

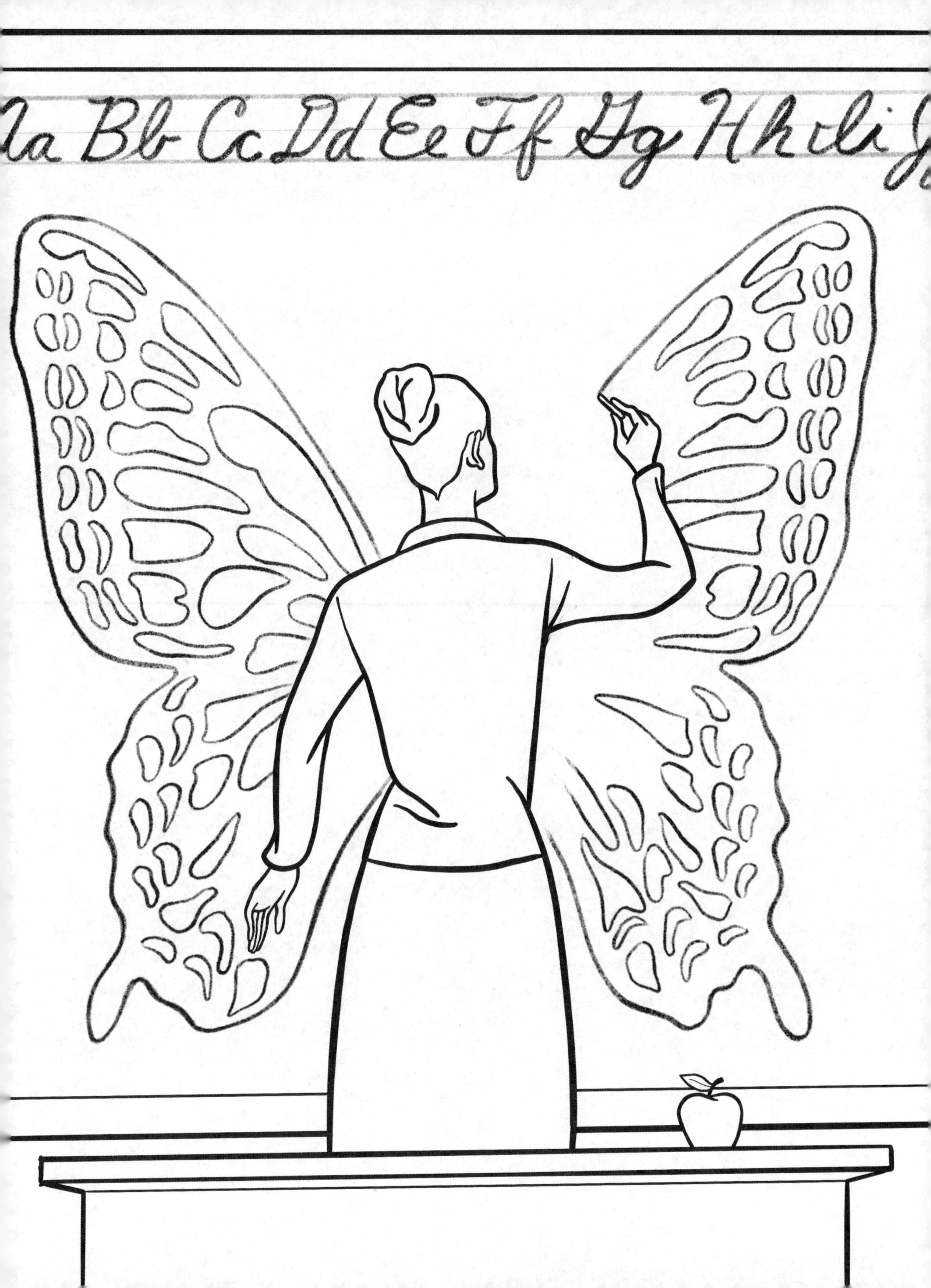
Bb Cc Dd Ee Ff Gg Hh Ii

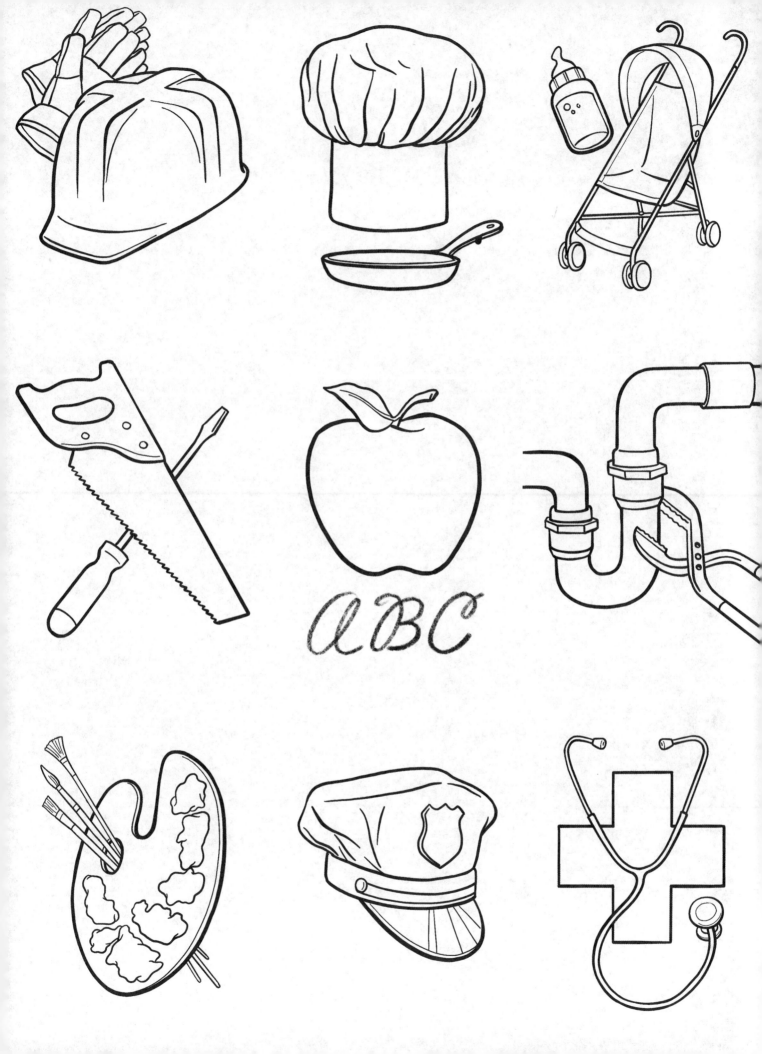

Draw and color your occupational strength.

Section 7
Environmental Health

Things you can do to improve environmental health

- Educate yourself about what can be done to safeguard the environment in the area where you live
- Teach family members and students how they can help
- Avoid doing things that would have a negative impact on the air, water, or land
- Become cognizant of how your daily habits affect the environment and make any changes that are necessary
- Protect yourself from environmental hazards
- Help others be aware of the earth's specific resources and limitations

Interesting Color Facts

The Impact Of Color On Physiology: Heart Rate And Blood Pressure · Color has been examined for its
impact on human physiology including changes in heart rate, respiratory rate, blood pressure, levels of arousal/alertness/ impulsivity, and the activation of the parasympathetic nervous system.   Although the effect is small, red typically has arousal effects and can raise your heart rate, while blue light can lower it. One study found that when the walls of a schoolroom were changed from orange and white to blue, the carpet changed from orange to light gray, and the fluorescent lights replaced with full-spectrum lighting, student behavior changed. Researchers observed that not only did children's mean systolic blood pressure drop from 120 to 100, but also that the children were better behaved, more attentive, less fidgety, and less aggressive. This suggests that there may be a physiological mechanism through which color and light can affect mood, heart rate, alertness, and impulsivity.

The Impact Of Color On Physiology: Impulsivity ·
Cities around the world have experimented with the impact of color on impulsive behavior by installing blue lights at the end of railway platforms or bridges in an attempt to reduce suicides and installing blue colored street lights in an attempt to reduce crime. Although it is hypothesized that blue light could make people less impulsive and more calm, there is not enough scientific evidence yet to support widespread adoption of these measures despite the fact that some cities have reported a 74% reduction in suicide rates.

Coloring Benefits

Art Therapy And Decreased PTSD Symptoms · Researchers have explored the effects of working with a therapist to create
Jungian mandalas on depression, anxiety, and PTSD symptoms. Although these mandalas are unstructured (consisting of free drawing in a circle instead of filling in a predetermined circular design with color) and are created under the supervision of a therapist, some researchers argue the results suggest the effectiveness of circular coloring and drawing for non-clinical populations due to the ways in which it helped decrease symptoms of PTSD for participants. More research in this area is needed to further explore potential applications and treatments.

Increased Self-Efficacy · Psychologists believe that a strong sense of self-efficacy is key to how we approach new challenges and
overcome disappointments in life. Realizing you can finish coloring a complicated design pattern may boost your sense of self-efficacy and help you better approach bigger challenges. In addition, seeing a finished product adorning your walls, or receiving praise from a loved one on your work can boost your self-confidence.

Color Corner

They're only crayons. You didn't fear them in Kindergarten, why fear them now?

Hugh MacLeod

Colors, like features, follow the changes of the emotions.

Pablo Picasso

Let me, O let me bathe my soul in colors; let me swallow the sunset and drink the rainbow.

Kahlil Gibran

Coloring Strategies To Try

Choose Your Coloring Books Wisely · The effect coloring can have on your mood can be altered by the type of coloring book you choose says Ikuko Acosta, director of the Graduate Art Therapy Program at NYU. "If the coloring book's images are very calm and soothing ... it might conjure up different feelings than one that's action-oriented, full of violence and movement," she explains. "It kind of sets up a certain emotional state for the artist." If you are looking to escape the grimy, urban jungle, an enchanted forest may be the perfect sort of world to dive into.

Start Simple · If you are just starting to color, keep things simple. Forget shading, burnishing, details, and texture and just start by block coloring (using your colored pencil to fill an area between the lines completely and evenly with that color). Producing a nice even color with your coloring pencil takes time and a focused attention on the pressure you are apply. Block coloring will help you master control and prime you for learning more advanced techniques.

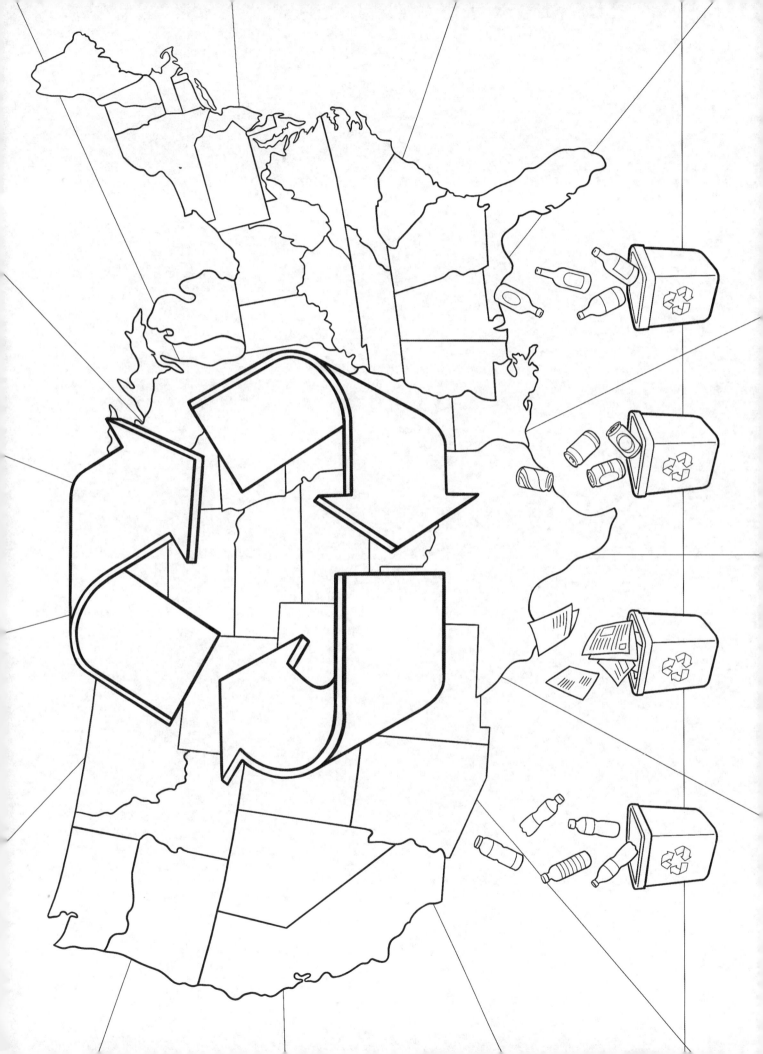

Draw and color your environmental strength.

Endnotes
Color Facts

Al-Ayash, A., Kane, R. T., Smith, D., & Green-Armytage, P. (2016). The influence of color on student emotion, heart rate, and performance in learning environments. Color Research and Application, 41 (2), 196-205.

Ault, A. (December 15, 2015). Ask Smithsonian: How do colors affect our moods? https://www.smithsonianmag.com/smithsonian-institution/ask-smithsonian-how-do-colors-affect-our-moods-180957504/

Azeemi, S. T. Y., & Raza, S. M. (2005). A critical analysis of chromotherapy and its scientific evolution. Evidence-Based Complementary and Alternative Medicine, 2 (4), 481-488.

Belluck, P. (February 5, 2009). Reinvent wheel? Blue room. Defusing a bomb? Red room. http://www.nytimes.com/2009/02/06/science/06color.html?_r=0

Berl, R. P. (March 24, 2015). Coloring books for grown-ups can ease stress and calm one's inner child. https://www.washingtonpost.com/express/wp/2015/03/24/coloring-books-for-grown-ups-can-ease-stress-and-calm-the-inner-child/?utm_term=.92ae09786ec5

Carolan, R., & Betts, D. (August 20, 2015). The adult coloring phenomenon: The American Art Therapy Association weighs in. https://3blmedia.com/News/Adult-Coloring-Book-Phenomenon

Cherry, K., & Gans, S. (February 24th, 2018). Color Psychology: Does it affect how your feel? https://www.verywellmind.com/color-psychology-2795824

Ciotti, G. (August 20, 2014). Color Psychology: How colors influence the mind. https://www.psychologytoday.com/blog/habits-not-hacks/201408/color-psychology-how-colors-influence-the-mind

Clydesdale, F. M. (1993). Color as a factor in food choice. Critical Reviews in Food Science and Nutrition, 33 (1), 83-101.

de Craen, A. J., Roos, P. J., de Vries, A. L., & Kleijnen, J. (1996). Effect of color of drugs: Systematic review of perceived effect of drugs and of their effectiveness. British Medical Journal, 313 (7072), 1624-1626.

Dovey, D. (October 8, 2015). The therapeutic science of adult coloring books: How this childhood pastime helps adults relieve stress. http://www.medicaldaily.com/therapeutic-science-adult-coloring-books-how-childhood-pastime-helps-adults-356280

Elliot, A. (2015). Color and psychological functioning: A review of theoretical and empirical work. Frontiers in Psychology, https://doi.org/10.3389/fpsyg.2015.00368.

Elliot, A. J., & Aarts, H. (2011). Perception of the color red enhances the force and velocity of motor output. Emotion, 11 (2), 445-449.

Elliott, A. J., & Maier, M. A. (2007). Color and psychological functioning. Current Directions in Psychological Sciences, 16 (5), 250-254.

Fairchild, M. D. (2013). Color Appearance Models. New York, NY: Wiley Press. doi: 10.1002/9781118653128

Frank, M. G., & Gillovich, T. (1988). The dark side of self and social perception: Black uniforms and aggression in professional sports. Journal of Personality and Social Psychology, 54 (1), 74-85.

Gao, et al. (2007). Analysis of cross-cultural color emotion. Color Research & Application, 32(3), 223 – 229.

Garber, L. L., Hyatt, E. M., & Starr, R. G (2000). The effects of food color on perceived flavor. The Journal of Marketing Theory and Practice, 8 (4), 59-72.

Gillan, K. (September 2, 2015). What's the science behind adult coloring-in books? https://coach.nine.com.au/2015/09/02/10/22/the-science-behind-adult-colouring-in-books

Gruson, L. (1982). Color has a powerful effect on behavior, researchers assert. https://www.nytimes.com/1982/10/19/science/color-has-a-powerful-effect-on-behavior-researchers-assert.html?pagewanted=all

Halzack, S. (March 12, 2016). The big business behind the adult coloring book craze. The Washington Post. https://www.washingtonpost.com/business/economy/the-big-business-behind-the-adult-coloring-book-craze/2016/03/09/ccf241bc-da62-11e5-891a-4ed04f4213e8_story.html?utm_term=.58f363ed4c99

Hill, R. A., & Barton, R. A. (2005). Psychology: Red enhances human performance in contests. Nature, 435, 293.

Jalil, N. A., Yunus, R. M., & Said, N. S. (2012). Environmental color impact upon human behavior: A review. Procedia - Social and Behavioral Sciences 35, 54-62.

Kaya, N., & Epps, H. H. (2004). Relationship between color and emotion: A study of college students. College Student Journal, 38 (3), 396-405.

Kuehni, R. (2012). Color: An Introduction to Practice and Principles. New York, NY: Wiley. doi: 10.1002/9781118533567

Kuller, R., Ballal, S., Laike, T. Mikellides, B., & Tonello, G. (2006). The impact of light and color on psychological mood: A cross-cultural study of indoor work environments. Ergonomics, 49 (14), 1496-1507.

Kurt, S., & Osueke, K. K. (2014). The effects of color on

the moods of college students. SAGE Open, January-March, 1-12.

Labrecque, L. I., & Milne, G. R. (2012). Exciting red and competent blue: The importance of color in marketing. Journal of the Academy of Marketing Science, 40 (5), 711-727.

Mantzios, M., & Giannou, K. (2018). When did coloring books become mindful? Exploring the effectiveness of a novel method of mindfulness-guided instructions for coloring books to increase mindfulness and decrease anxiety. Frontiers in Psychology, 9, (56).

McAffee, M. (April 24, 2015). Adult coloring books topping best seller lists. https://www.cnn.com/2015/04/21/living/feat-adult-coloring-books/index.html

Mehta, R., & Zhu, R. (2009). Blue or red? Exploring the effect of color on cognitive task performances. Science, 323 (5918), 1226-1229.

Ridgeway, J., & Meyers, B. (2014). A study on brand personality: Consumers' perceptions of colors used in fashion brand logos. International Journal of Fashion Design, Technology and Education, 7 (1), 50.

Soldat, A. S., Sinclair, R. C., & Mark, M. M. (1997). Color as an environmental processing cue. Social Cognition, 15 (1), 55-71.

Spence, C., Velasco, C., & Knoeferle, K. (2014). A large sample study on the influence of the multisensory environment on the wine drinking experience. Flavour, 3, 8. https://doi.org/10.1186/2044-7248-3-8

Storebele, N., & De Castro, J. M. (2004). Effect of ambience on food intake and food choice. Nutrition, 20 (9), 821-838.

Wadhera, D., & Capaldi-Phillips, E. D. (2014). A review of visual cues associated with food on food acceptance and consumption. Eating Behaviors, 15 (1), 132-143.

Walsh, L. M., Toma, R. B., Tuveson, R. V., & Sondhi, L. (1990). Color preference and food choice among children. The Journal of Psychology, 124 (6), 645-653.

Westland, S. (September 30, 2017). Here's How Colors Really Affect Our Brain and Body, According to Science. https://www.sciencealert.com/does-colour-really-affect-our-brain-and-body-a-professor-of-colour-science-explains

Wikipedia. https://en.wikipedia.org/wiki/Chromotherapy

Color Benefits

Alter, A. (March 30, 2013). Grown-ups get out their crayons. https://www.nytimes.com/2015/03/30/business/media/grown-ups-get-out-their-crayons.html?_r=1

Archer, S., Buxton, S., & Sheffield, D. (2015). The effect of creative psychological intervention on psychological outcomes for adult cancer patients: A systematic review of randomized controlled trials. Psychooncology, 24, 1-10.

Babouchkina A., & Robbins S. J. (2015). Reducing negative mood through mandala creation: A randomized controlled trial. Art Therapy, 32, 34–39. 10.1080/07421656.2015.994428

Brown, K. W., Ryan, R. M., & Creswell, J. D. (2007). Mindfulness: Theoretical foundations and evidence for its salutary effects. Psychological Inquiry, 18 (4), 211-237.

Carolan, R., & Betts, D. (August 20, 2015). The adult coloring phenomenon: The American art therapy association weighs in. https://3blmedia.com/News/Adult-Coloring-Book-Phenomenon

Carsley, D., Heath, N. L., & Fajnerova, S. (2015). Effectiveness of a classroom mindfulness coloring activity for test anxiety in children. Journal of Applied School Psychology, 31, 239-255.

Clarke, K., & Morrow, L. (2016). Kidding around: Using play to enhance students' well-being and learning. Pacific North-West Library Association Quarterly, 81 (1), 32-40.

Clift, C. (April 29, 2015). Here's what happens when you color instead of watch TV for a week. https://www.brit.co/my-week-coloring-book-adults/

Comfortable Shoes Studio (2015). Opinion: Adult coloring books and art therapy. http://comfortableshoesstudio.com/opinion-adult-coloring-books-and-art-therapy/

Cox, C. T., & Cohen, B. M. (2000). Mandala artwork by clients with DID: Clinical observations based on two theoretical models. Journal of the American Art Therapy Association, 17 (3), 195-201.

Couch, J. B. (1997). Behind the veil: Mandala drawings by dementia patients. Journal of the American Art Therapy Association, 14 (3), 187-193.

Csikszentmihalyi, M. (1990). Flow: The Psychology of Optimal Performance. New York, NY: Cambridge University Press.

Csikszentmihalyi, M. (2004). Flow, the secret to happiness. https://www.ted.com/talks/mihaly_csikszentmihalyi_on_flow

Curry, N. A., & Kasser, T. (2005). Can coloring mandalas reduce anxiety? Art Therapy, 22, 81–85. 10.1080/10615806.2015.1076798

DeLue, C. (1999). Physiological effects of creating mandalas. In C. Malchiodi (Ed.), Medical Art Therapy with Children (pp. 33-49). London: Jessica Kingsley Publishers Ltd.).

Dovey, D. (October 8, 2015). The therapeutic science of

adult coloring books: How this childhood pastime helps adults relieve stress. http://www.medicaldaily.com/therapeutic-science-adult-coloring-books-how-childhood-pastime-helps-adults-356280

Drake, C. R., Searight, H. R., & Olson-Pupek, K. (2014). The influence of art-making on negative mood states in university students. American Journal of Applied Psychology, 2(3), 69-72.

Drake, J. E., & Winner, E. (2012). Confronting sadness through art-making: Distraction is more beneficial than venting. Psychology of Aesthetics, Creativity and the Arts, 6(3), 255-261. doi: 10.1037/a0026909

Fitzpatrick, K. (August 1, 2017). Why adult coloring books are good for you. https://www.cnn.com/2016/01/06/health/adult-coloring-books-popularity-mental-health/index.html

Flett, J. A., Lie, C., Riordin, B. C., Thompson, L. M., Conner, T. S., & Hayne, H. (2017). Sharpen your pencils: Preliminary evidence that adult coloring reduces depressive symptoms and anxiety. Creativity Research Journal, 29 (4), 409-416.

Fornazzari, L., Ringer, T., Ringer, L., & Fischer, C. E. (2013). Preserved drawing in a sculptor with dementia. The Canadian Journal of Neurological Sciences, 40, 736-737.

Frank, P. (July 28, 2015). Why coloring could be the new alternative to meditation. https://www.huffingtonpost.com/entry/coloring-benefits-meditation_us_55b7c9c1e4b0074ba5a6724f

Fredrickson, B. L., Cohn, M. A., Coffey, K. A., Pek, J., & Finkel, S. M. (2008). Open hearts build lives: Positive emotions, induced through loving-kindness meditation, build consequential personal resources. Journal of Personality and Social Psychology, 95, 1045-1062.

Geda, Y. E., Topazian, H. M., Roberts, R. O., Knopman, D. S., Pankratz, V. S., Christainson, T. J., Boeve, B. F., Tangalos, E. G., Ivnik, R. J., & Petersen, R. C. (2011). Engaging in cognitive activates, aging, and mild cognitive impairment: A population-based study. The Journal of Neuropsychiatry and Clinical Neurosciences, 23 (2), 149-154.

Gillan, K. (September 2, 2015). What's the science behind adult coloring-in books? https://coach.nine.com.au/2015/09/02/10/22/the-science-behind-adult-colouring-in-books

Gutman, S. A., & Schindler, V. P. (2007). The neurological basis of occupation. Occupational Therapy International, 14 (2), 71-85.

Hall, K. (n. d.). Self-soothing: Calming the amygdala and reducing the effects of trauma. https://blogs.psychcentral.com/emotionally-sensitive/2012/04/self-soothing-calming-the-amgydala/

Halzack, S. (March 12, 2016). The big business behind the adult coloring book craze. The Washington Post. https://www.washingtonpost.com/business/economy/the-big-business-behind-the-adult-coloring-book-craze/2016/03/09/ccf241bc-da62-11e5-891a-4ed04f4213e8_story.html?utm_term=.58f363ed4c99

Hanley, A. W., Warner, A. R., Dehili, V. M., Canto, A. I., & Garland, E. L. (2015). Washing dishes to wash the dishes: Brief instruction in an informal mindfulness practice. Mindfulness, 6, 1095-1103.

Henderson P., Rosen, D., & Mascaro, N. (2007). Empirical study on the healing nature of mandalas. Psychology of Aesthetics, Creativity, and the Arts (1), 148–154. 10.1037/1931-3896.1.3.148

Kajmal, G., Ray, K., & Munia, J. (2016). Reduction of cortisol levels and participants' responses following art making. Journal of the American Art Therapy Association, 33 (2), 74-80.

Lawson, L. M., Williams, P., Glennon, C., Carithers, K., Schnabel, E., Andrejack, A., & Wright, N. (2012). Effect of art making on cancer-related symptoms of blood and marrow transplantation recipients. Oncology Nursing Forum, 39(4), E353–E360. doi:10.1188/12.ONF.E353-E360

Mantzios, M. & Giannou, K. (2018). When did coloring books become mindful? Exploring the effectiveness of a novel method of mindfulness-guided instructions for coloring books to increase mindfulness and decrease anxiety. Frontiers in Psychology, 9, (56).

Martinez, N. (November 24, 2015). Reasons adult coloring books are great for our mental, emotional and intellectual health. https://www.huffingtonpost.com/dr-nikki-martinez-psyd-lcpc/7-reasons-adult-coloring-books-are-great-for-your-mental-emotional-and-intellectual-health_b_8626136.html

Metcalf, E. (n.d.) Make time for play. https://www.webmd.com/balance/features/fun-play#1

Monson, N. (November 14, 2015). Why the latest coloring-book craze can be good for you. https://www.usatoday.com/story/life/books/2015/11/14/why-latest-coloring-book-craze-can-good-you/75723218/

Monti, D. A., Peterson, C., Kunkel, E . J., Hauck, W. W., Pequignot, E., Rhodes, L., & Brainard, G. C. (2006). A randomized, controlled trial of mindfulness-based art therapy (MBAT) for women with cancer. Psychooncology, 15 (5), 363-373.

Nainis, N., Paice, J. A., Ratner, J. Wirth, J. H., Lai, J., & Shott, S. (2006). Relieving symptoms in cancer: Innovative use of art therapy. Journal of Pain and Symptom Management 31 (2), 162-169.

Olesen, J. (n.d.). Ten therapeutic benefits of coloring books for adults. https://www.color-meanings.com/10-

therapeutic-benefits-of-coloring-books-for-adults/

Pisarik, C. T., & Larson, K. R. (2011). Facilitating college students' authenticity and psychological well-being through the use of mandalas: An empirical study. The Journal of Humanistic Counselling, 50, 84-98.

Potash, J. S., Chen, J. Y., Tsang, J. P. Y. (2015). Medical student mandala making for holistic well-being. Medical Humanities, 42, 17–25. 10.1136/medhum-2015-010717

Proyer, R. T., & Wagner, L. (2015). Playfulness in adults revisited: The signal theory in German speakers. American Journal of Play, 7 (2), 201-227.

Puig, A., Lee, S. M., Goodwin, L., & Sherrard, P. A. D. (2006). The efficacy of creative arts therapies to enhance emotional expression, spirituality, and psychological well-being of newly diagnosed Stage I and Stage II breast cancer patients: A preliminary study. The Arts in Psychotherapy, 33(3), 218–228.

Reynolds, F., & Prior, S. (2003). A lifestyle coat-hanger: A phenomenological study of the meanings of artwork for women coping with chronic illness. Disability Rehabilitation, 25(14), 785–794. doi:10.1080/0963828031000093486

Reynolds, M. W., & Lim, K. H. (2007). Contribution of visual art-making to the subjective well-being of women living with cancer: A qualitative study. The Arts in Psychotherapy, 34(1), 1–10.

Rigby, M., & Taubert, M. (2016). Art of medicine: Coloring books for adults on the cancer ward. British Medical Journal, 352. h6795 10.1136.

Riley, J., Corkhill, B., & Morris, C. (2013). The benefits of knitting for personal and social wellbeing in adulthood: Findings from an international survey. British Journal of Occupational Therapy, 76 (2), 50-57.

Ross, E. A., Hollen, T. L., & Fitzgerald, B. M. (2006). Observational study of an arts-in-medicine program in an outpatient hemodialysis unit. American Journal of Kidney Disease, 47 (3), 462-468.

Samoray, J. (2006). The healing effects of creative expression experienced by people who identify themselves as having compassion fatigue: A phenomenological study. Dissertation Abstracts International: Section B: Sciences and Engineering, 66(9B), 5103.

Sandmire, D. A., Rankin, N. E., Gorham, S. R., Eggleston, D. T., French, C. A., Lodge, E. E., Kuns, G. C., & Grimm, D. R. (2015). Psychological and autonomic effects of art making in college-aged students. Anxiety, Stress, & Coping, 29 (5), 561-569.

Santos, E. (October 13, 2014). Coloring isn't just for kids. It can actually help adults combat stress. https://www.huffingtonpost.com/2014/10/13/coloring-for-stress_n_5975832.html

Schwedel, H. (2015). Coloring books for adults: We asked therapists for their opinions. https://www.theguardian.com/lifeandstyle/2015/aug/17/coloring-books-adults-therapists-opinions

Smitherman-Brown, V., & Church, R. P. (1996). Mandala drawing: Facilitating creative growth in children with ADD or ADHD. Art Therapy: Journal of the American Art Therapy Association, 13, 252-262.

Stuckey, H. L., & Nobel, J. (2010). The connection between art, healing and public health: A review of current literature. American Journal of Public Health, 100 (2), 254-263.

van der Vennet R., & Serice S. (2012). Can coloring mandalas reduce anxiety? A replication study. Art Therapy, 29, 87–92. 10.1080/10615806.2015.1076798

Walsh, S. M., Chang, C. Y., Schmidt, L. A., & Yoepp, J. H. (2004). Lowering stress while teaching research: A creative arts intervention in the classroom. Journal of Nursing Education, 44 (7), 330-333.

Walsh, S. M., Martin, S. C., & Schmidt, L. A. (2004). Testing the efficacy of a creative-arts intervention with family caregivers of patients with cancer. Journal of Nursing Scholarship, 36 (3), 214-219.

Walsh, S. M., Radcliffe, S., Castillo, S., Kumar, A., & Broschard, D. (2007). A pilot-study to test the effects of art-making classes for family caregivers of patients with cancer. Oncology Nursing Forum, 34, E9–E16. doi:10.1188/07.ONF.E9-E16

Weller, C. (August 26, 2013). Art therapy and dementia: How creativity helps unlock Alzheimer's patients' thoughts and fears. http://www.medicaldaily.com/art-therapy-and-dementia-how-creativity-helps-unlock-alzheimers-patients-thoughts-and-fears-254301

Wilson, J. (January 5, 2015). This is your brain on crafting. https://www.cnn.com/2014/03/25/health/brain-crafting-benefits/index.html

Wilson, K. (August 4, 2015). 7 Reasons adult coloring books will make your life a whole lot brighter. https://www.bustle.com/articles/101264-7-reasons-adult-coloring-books-will-make-your-life-a-whole-lot-brighter

Color Strategies

Clift, C. (April 29, 2015). Here's what happens when you color instead of watch TV for a week. https://www.brit.co/my-week-coloring-book-adults/

Notes:

Record two actions you will take to improve each dimension of wellness.

Physical

1.

2.

Emotional

1.

2.

Intellectual

1.

2.

Social

1.

2.

Spiritual

1.

2.

Occupational

IN   OUT

1.

2.

Environmental

1.

2.